# EXPLORING
# THE ROCK CYCLE

## PETROLOGISTS AT WORK!

### ELSIE OLSON

Consulting Editor, Diane Craig, M.A./Reading Specialist

**Super Sandcastle**

An Imprint of Abdo Publishing
abdopublishing.com

# abdopublishing.com

Published by Abdo Publishing, a division of ABDO, PO Box 398166, Minneapolis, Minnesota 55439. Copyright © 2018 by Abdo Consulting Group, Inc. International copyrights reserved in all countries. No part of this book may be reproduced in any form without written permission from the publisher. Super SandCastle™ is a trademark and logo of Abdo Publishing.

Printed in the United States of America, North Mankato, Minnesota

102017
012018

THIS BOOK CONTAINS
RECYCLED MATERIALS

Design: Kelly Doudna, Mighty Media, Inc.
Production: Mighty Media, Inc.
Editor: Jessie Alkire
Cover Photographs: iStockphoto; Shutterstock; Wikimedia Commons
Interior Photographs: iStockphoto; NASA; Sean Smith/NASA; Shutterstock; Wikimedia Commons

Publisher's Cataloging-in-Publication Data

Names: Olson, Elsie, author.
Title: Exploring the rock cycle: petrologists at work! / by Elsie Olson.
Other titles: Petrologists at work!
Description: Minneapolis, Minnesota : Abdo Publishing, 2018. | Series: Earth detectives |
Identifiers: LCCN 2017946442 | ISBN 9781532112324 (lib.bdg.) | ISBN 9781614799740 (ebook)
Subjects: LCSH: Petrology--Juvenile literature. | Geochemical cycles--Juvenile literature. |
    Occupations--Juvenile literature. | Earth sciences--Juvenile literature.
Classification: DDC 552--dc23
LC record available at https://lccn.loc.gov/2017946442

Super SandCastle™ books are created by a team of professional educators, reading specialists, and content developers around five essential components—phonemic awareness, phonics, vocabulary, text comprehension, and fluency—to assist young readers as they develop reading skills and strategies and increase their general knowledge. All books are written, reviewed, and leveled for guided reading, early reading intervention, and Accelerated Reader™ programs for use in shared, guided, and independent reading and writing activities to support a balanced approach to literacy instruction.

# CONTENTS

What Is the Rock Cycle? 4

Who Studies the Rock Cycle? 6

James Hutton 8

Ancient Earth 10

Petrologists at Work 12

In the Field and Lab 14

Changing Earth 16

A Petrologist's Tool Kit 18

Out of This World 20

Become a Petrologist! 22

Test Your Knowledge 23

Glossary 24

# WHAT IS THE ROCK CYCLE?

The rock cycle is a **geologic** process. It tells how rocks are formed, changed, and destroyed. Rocks are combinations of minerals. Minerals are nonliving **substances** in nature.

There are three types of rocks. Igneous rocks form when **magma** cools and hardens. Sedimentary rocks form when **sediment** builds up. The sediment **compacts** into rock. Metamorphic rocks were once different kinds of rock. Heat and pressure changed them.

SEDIMENTARY ROCK

HEAT AND PRESSURE

MELTING

COMPACTING

SEDIMENT

MAGMA

EROSION

HARDENING

MELTING

EROSION

HEAT AND PRESSURE

METAMORPHIC ROCK

IGNEOUS ROCK

# WHO STUDIES THE ROCK CYCLE?

Petrologists are scientists. They study rocks. Petrologists look at how rocks are formed. They study what rocks are made of.

This work is important. It teaches us about processes that shape Earth. It can tell us what Earth was like long ago.

*Sedimentary rock*

# JAMES HUTTON

James Hutton was a petrologist. He is called the founder of modern **geology**. James lived in Scotland in the 1700s.

James went to college when he was 14! He studied science and math. He also studied medicine. James farmed after college. He studied soil and rocks on his land. He traveled to study other rocks.

*Scottish Highlands*

James was a wise observer of the world around him. He studied rocks closely and formed arguments and conclusions based on reason.

# ANCIENT EARTH

Hutton realized that different rocks form in different ways. He came up with a rock cycle. Rocks are formed, changed, and destroyed in the cycle. But the cycle takes a long time.

*Sandstone*

At the time, people thought Earth was 6,000 years old. Hutton realized it was much older. Not everyone agreed with Hutton's ideas. But scientists later accepted his **theories**.

# JAMES HUTTON

**BORN:** June 3, 1726, Edinburgh, Scotland

**MARRIED:** Never married

**CHILDREN:** James Smeaton Hutton (circa 1747)

**DIED:** March 26, 1797, Edinburgh, Scotland

# PETROLOGISTS AT WORK

Scientists continue Hutton's work. **Petrology** has three main branches. There is a branch for each type of rock.

Petrologists look at the minerals rocks are made of. Some rocks have one type of mineral. Others have many types. Scientists know of more than 4,000 minerals!

Petrologists learn how we can use rocks in our daily lives. Rocks can be turned into materials used in construction and other industries.

# IN THE FIELD AND LAB

Petrologists travel the world. They collect rock samples. Then they study samples in labs.

Petrologists look at a rock's texture. They study the size of its grains. They learn what minerals the rock is made of. Then the scientists **classify** the rock.

*Mineral samples*

Some petrologists work for governments or mining companies. Petrologists find out if an area or its rock contains valuable or beneficial natural resources.

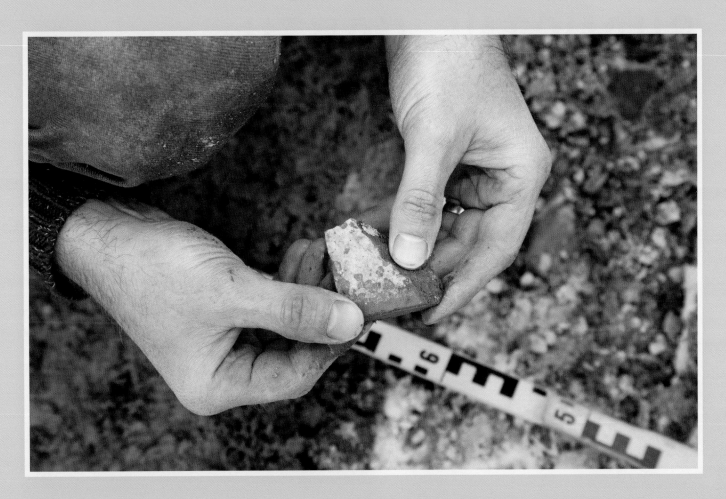

# CHANGING EARTH

Scientists study where different rocks form. This tells scientists about the **geologic** history of an area. These studies also tell scientists how an area's rocks have changed.

Some rocks are formed and shaped within Earth. Others are changed on Earth's surface. Heat and pressure change rocks. So do wind, water, and weather. These processes can cause **erosion**.

Learning about these processes is important. It helps scientists understand how Earth might change in the future.

Studying rocks helps scientists learn what Earth's surface is made of. This teaches them about activity below Earth's surface. This activity can cause natural disasters, such as volcanoes.

# A PETROLOGIST'S TOOL KIT

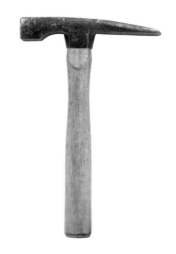

## GPS
**GPS** devices map where rocks were found.

## ROCK HAMMER
This tool is used to break open rocks.

Petrologists use many tools to collect and study rocks.

## PETROGRAPHIC MICROSCOPE
This lets scientists examine rocks up close. The scientists can see what minerals the rocks are made of.

## X-RAY FLUORESCENCE SPECTROMETER
This **X-ray** instrument scans rocks. It tells what chemicals are in rocks.

# OUT OF THIS WORLD

**Petrology** is an exciting science. Some rocks hold valuable minerals. Scientists learn how to remove the minerals.

Petrologists also study rocks from outer space. **Meteorites** tell scientists what planets and asteroids are made of. These rocks contain the same minerals as Earth's rocks. Scientists also study moon rocks. These tell us about the early history of the moon!

Astronauts went to the moon in 1969. They brought back moon rocks. One moon rock now sits on the International Space Station.

# BECOME A PETROLOGIST!

Do you dream of becoming a petrologist? Here are some things you can do now!

**TAKE SCIENCE AND MATH CLASSES.** Studying the rock cycle involves math and science. Getting good grades in those classes now will help you in the future.

**PRACTICE YOUR COMPUTER SKILLS.** Petrologists do much of their work on computers. They must learn special computer programs.

**ASK QUESTIONS!** Scientists ask a lot of questions. They look for new ways to find answers. You can get started now!

# TEST YOUR KNOWLEDGE

1. Igneous rocks are formed from cooled and hardened **magma**. TRUE OR FALSE?

2. How old was James Hutton when he went to college?

3. How many minerals do scientists know of?

## THINK ABOUT IT!

Have you ever picked up a rock outside? How do you think it formed?

ANSWERS: 1. True 2. 14 3. More than 4,000

# GLOSSARY

**classify** – to put things in groups according to their characteristics.

**compact** – to press together.

**erosion** – the wearing away of land or rocks, especially by wind or water.

**geology** – the science of Earth and its structure.

**magma** – melted rock below Earth's surface.

**meteorite** – a space object that hits the surface of the earth.

**petrology** – the study of rocks.

**sediment** – matter, such as rocks, that is deposited by water, wind, or glaciers.

**substance** – anything that takes up space, such as a solid object or a liquid.

**theory** – an idea that explains how or why something happens.

**X-ray** – an invisible and powerful light wave that can pass through solid objects.